INTERIOR DESIGN
Mood Board
KIDS EDITION
Girls

Create Your Interior Design Mood Board!
In this Book, You will find 35 pages with
over 240 elements to cut out and 15 empty
templates for your collage.

Cut Out- Furniture and Decor

Cut Out- Furniture and Decor

Cut Out- Furniture and Decor

Cut Out- Furniture and Decor

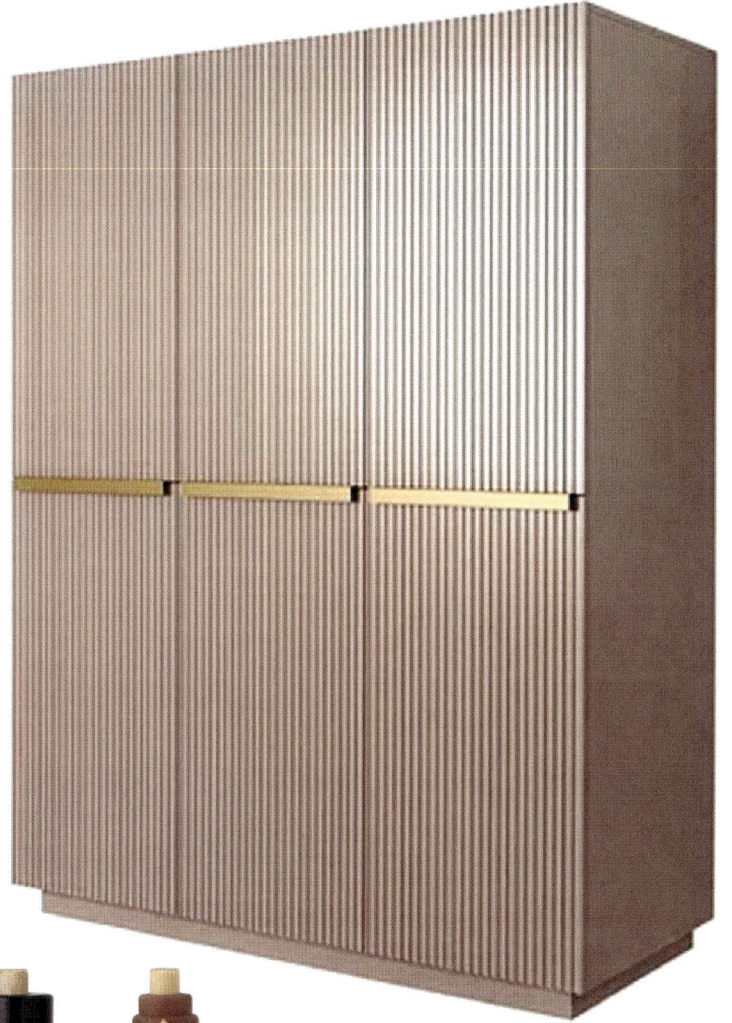

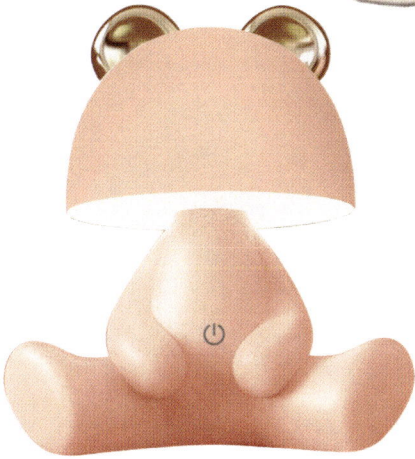

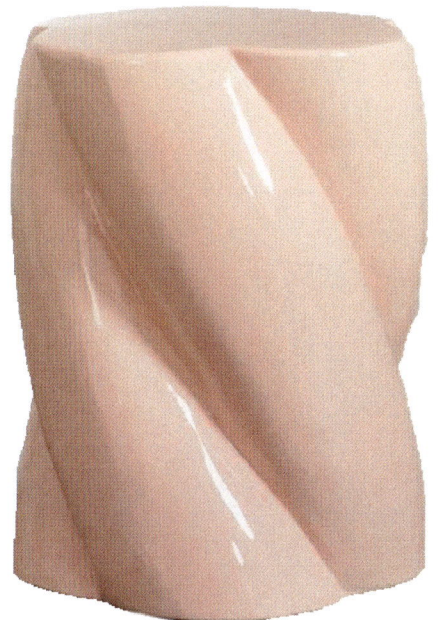

Cut Out- Furniture and Decor

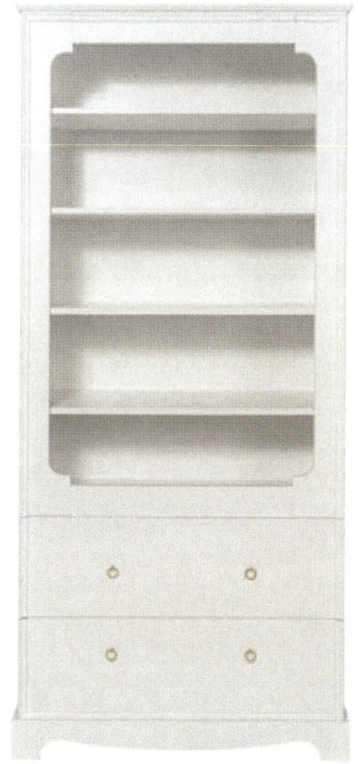

Cut Out- Furniture and Decor

Cut Out- Furniture and Decor

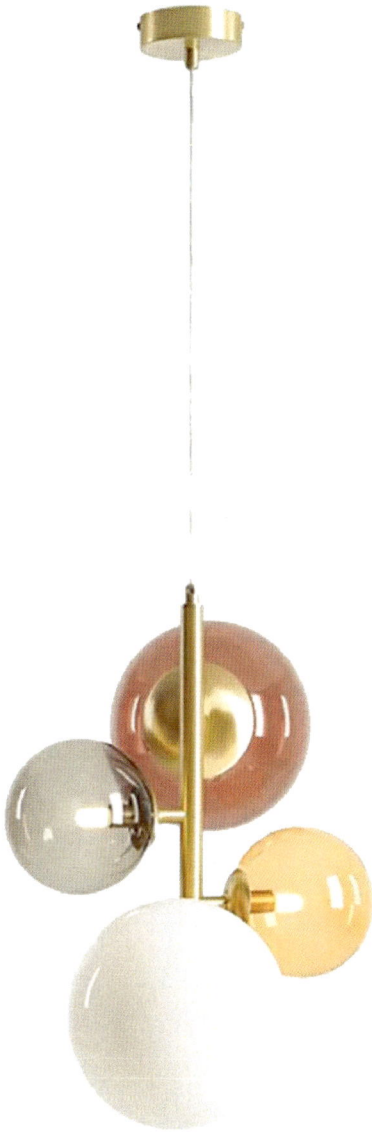

Cut Out- Furniture and Decor

Cut Out- Furniture and Decor

Cut Out- Furniture and Decor

Cut Out- Furniture and Decor

Cut Out- Furniture and Decor

Cut Out- Furniture and Decor

Cut Out- Furniture and Decor

Cut Out- Furniture and Decor

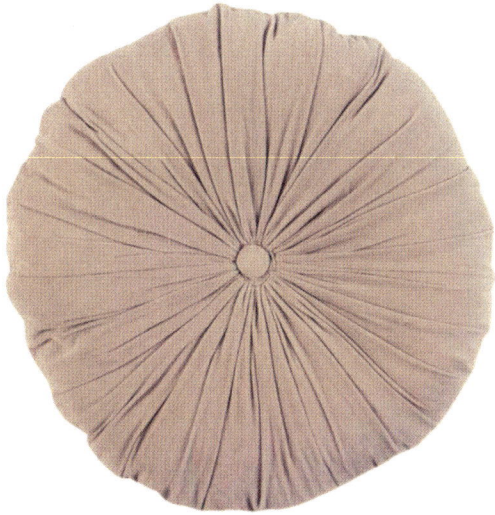

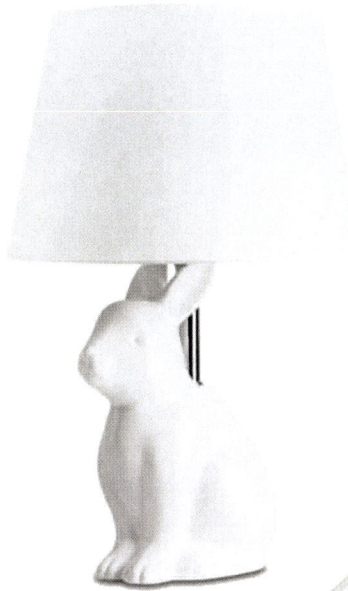

Cut Out- Furniture and Decor

Cut Out- Furniture and Decor

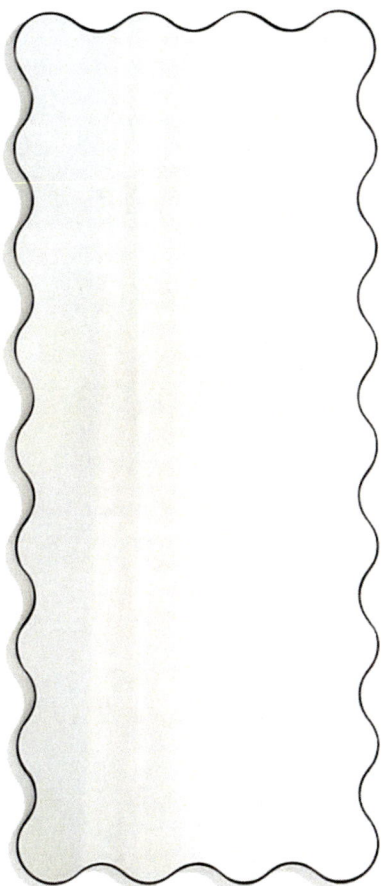

Cut Out- Furniture and Decor

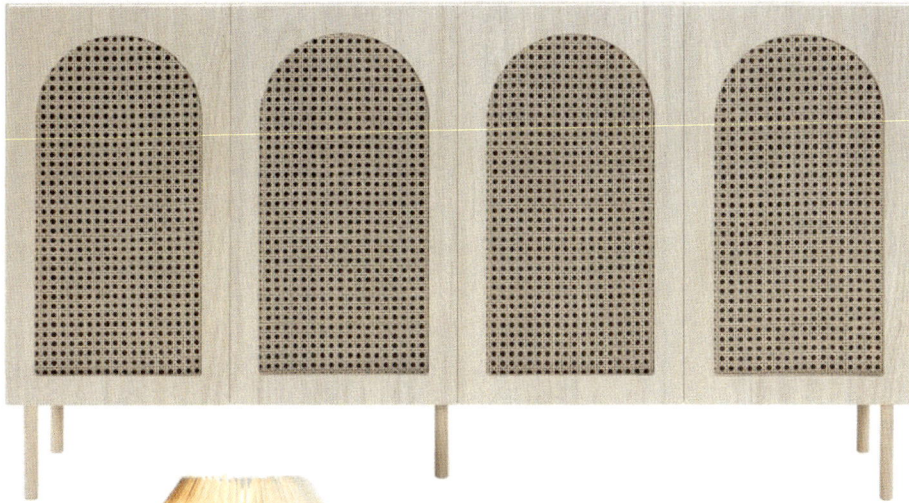

Cut Out- Furniture and Decor

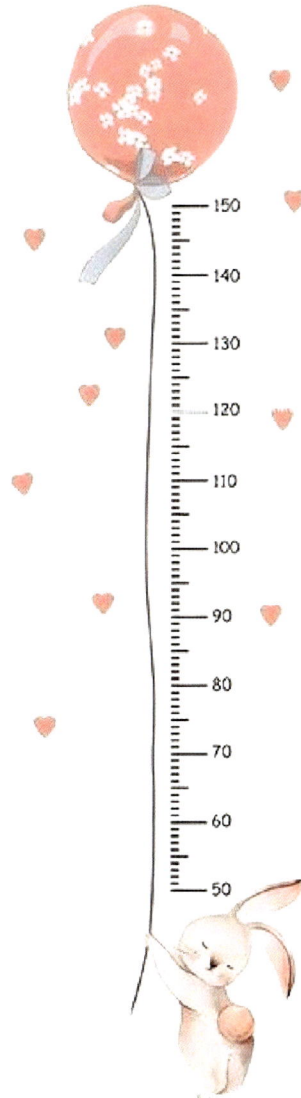

Cut Out- Furniture and Decor

Cut Out- Furniture and Decor

Cut Out- Furniture and Decor

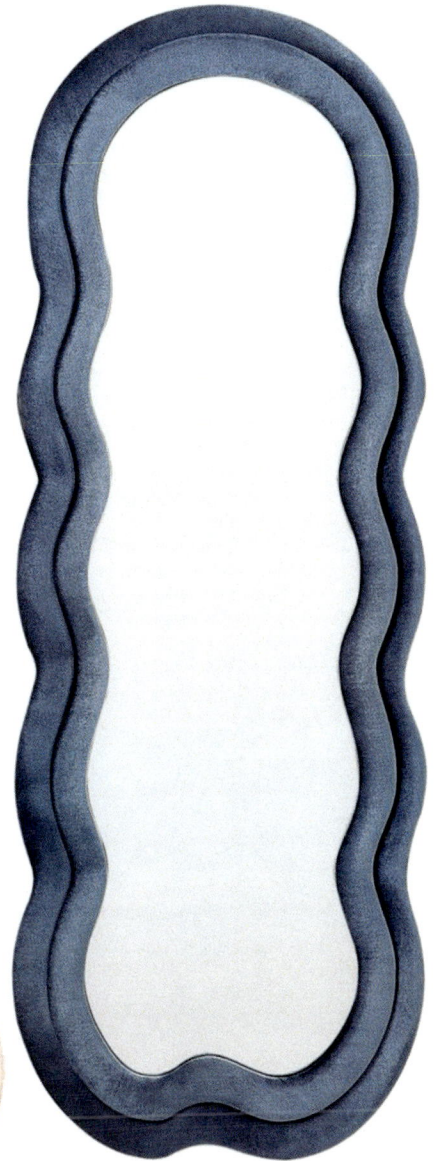

NO
TRESPASSING

GIRLS
ONLY

NO BOYS
ALLOWED

Cut Out- Furniture and Decor

Cut Out- Furniture and Decor

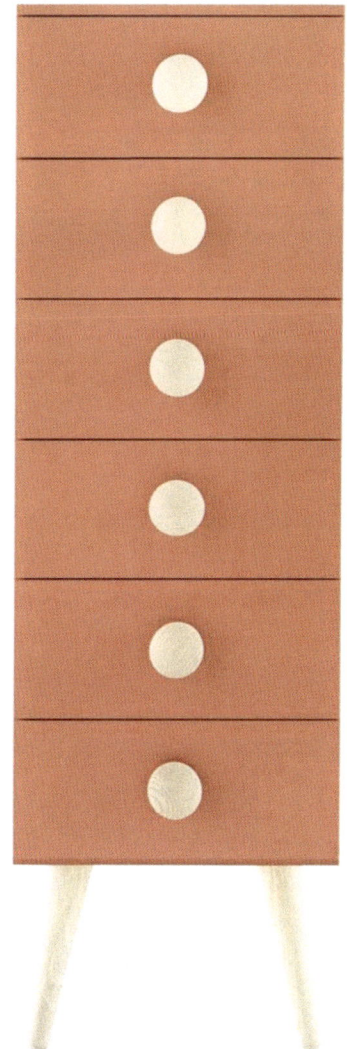

Cut Out- Furniture and Decor

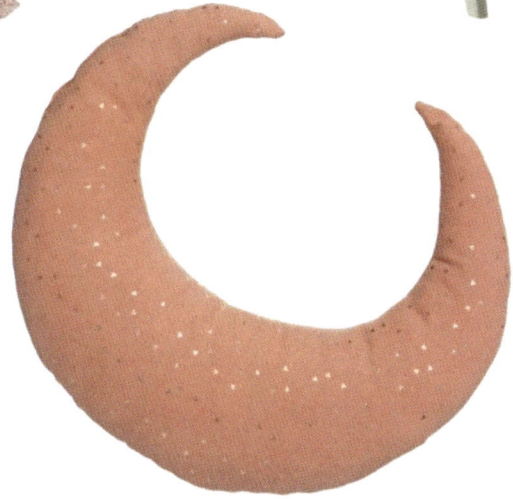

Cut Out- Furniture and Decor

Cut Out- Furniture and Decor

Cut Out- Furniture and Decor

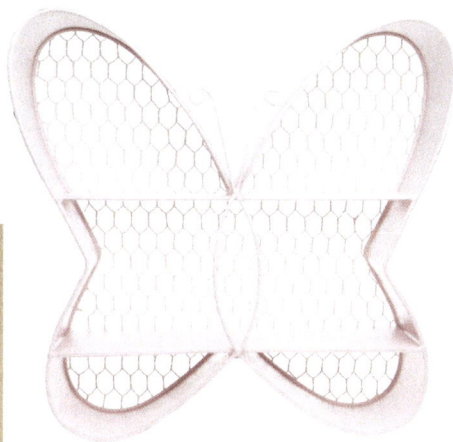

Cut Out- Furniture and Decor

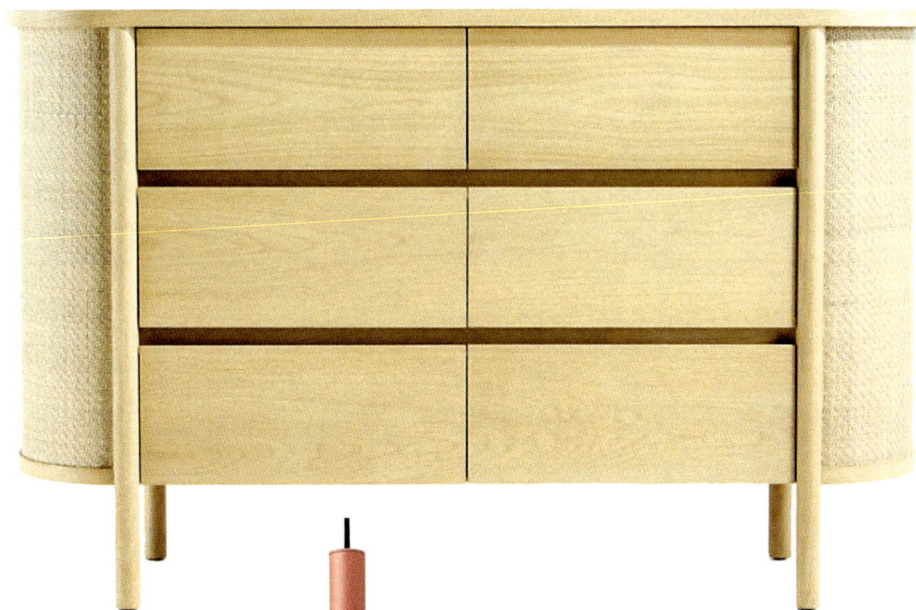

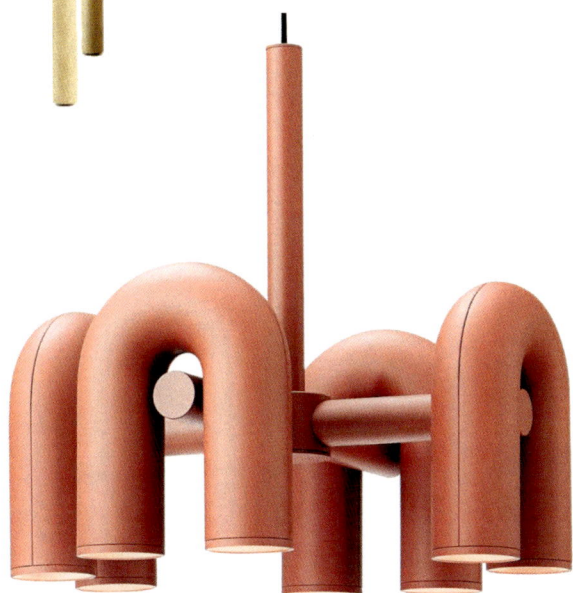

Cut Out- Furniture and Decor

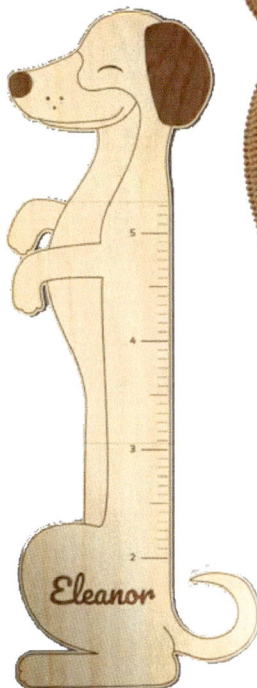

Cut Out- Wallpapers

Cut Out- Wallpapers

Cut Out- Wallpapers

Cut Out- Colors

Cut Out- Colors

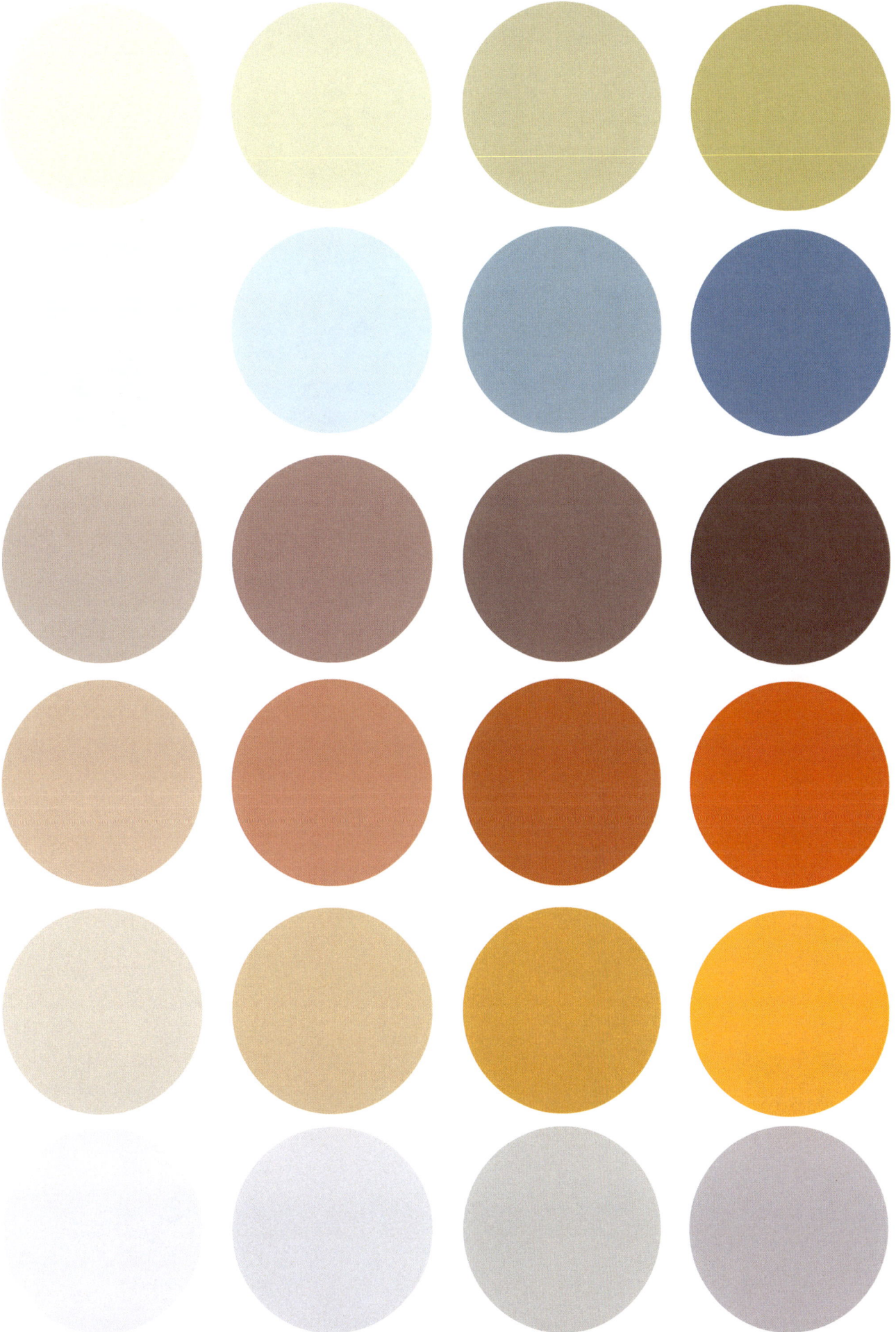

.... Mood Board

.... Mood Board

.... Mood Board

.... Mood Board

.... Mood Board

.... Mood Board

.... Mood Board

.... Mood Board

.... Mood Board

.... *Mood Board*

.... Mood Board

.... Mood Board

Made in United States
Orlando, FL
10 July 2025